# "Restored"

*A Journey through Adoption and Mental Health that lead to My Purpose*

**Jeremiah Isaiah Cain**

# Table of Contents

This book is dedicated to My mother who I've known personally from the beginning. For obeying the Will of God and taking me in, adopting me. I love you MaMa. Also, to an Angel, my biological mother whom I've never met but I know she loved me and is looking down on me proud.

This Angel in heaven reminding me to "Stay Sweet".

Mom Loves you so very much Jeremiah, I might go back to work (part time) at the Department of Natural Resources on Dr. Martin L King Jr Drive / north dae I will remember in a couple of weeks. I have a career secretary degree from Bauder...

Stay Sweet ... Hi Jeremiah

I am writing to Judge Standley Chaper for...

NOTE: Ms. Mary Garry (my "Tuiiti Fauiti")

Ms. Charley please bring my baby Jeremiah to see me here. The judge did order physical contact as michaes possible when you come - please ask for Catherine Williams (sister) to visit with Jeremiah please. He sends love & warmth.

May God keep and Bless you until we meet again in my arms daily

NOTE: I still want some pictures of my baby please - Thank you so very kindly.

Mom Loves you and I Miss you daily. Will see you real soon. OX-OX-OX (Hugs & Kisses)
Love,
— Hattie

# Introduction

The initial purpose of this book is to encourage everyone to tell your story. I mean, just get everything out of you. I was inspired to write this book to pour out what I have in me and to take you on a purposeful journey. A journey you've never been on before. It's a journey of my life and, for some, my testimony of being *"restored"*. It is a story of me growing up as an adopted child who was gifted. A gifted child who graduated from the school system and began a career in technology. After years of a successful career in IT (Information Technology), I found and reconnected with my biological family. Shortly after, I stumbled across a mental health diagnosis. I went through this ordeal, which was years of bondage. Eventually, I found a way to escape and overcome my problems. All this helped bring me closer to my purpose.

# Prelude

My life changed drastically the day I got home from the UFC gym, where I thought I had found my peace and ultimate meditation. Out of boredom and curiosity I had decided to pull out my adoption records to look them over again. As I got ready to put the papers away, I was surprised to see a page I had never seen before. It read in summary: Jeremiah Askew Cain has a mental health disorder. My world was absolutely shaken. As far as I knew, I was completely healthy because I thought I had been raised in a pretty healthy family. I had also been a successful IT Specialist in Cyber Security. So, a mental health diagnosis just didn't seem to fit.

I saw a psychiatrist who agreed with this diagnosis, which made it a concrete reality in my mind. Everything began to spin out of control, and the mental stability I thought I possessed no longer seemed to be a reality. After a few years of perpetuating mental bondage ranging from ADHD to Bipolar to Psychosis episodes where I imitated animals and insects publicly, I found a way of escaping and overcoming my mental issues. This experience helped bring me closer to walking in my purpose.

*Chapter 1*

# A Blessing in Disguise

I'm taking things back to my roots. Ms. Hattie Carter, my biological mother, a loving mother, struggled intensely with members of her family, mainly because of her resistance to their interventions and many attempts to help her loosen the tight grip of her cocaine addiction. Although she had struggles, many have described her humanity as being very funny, being a jokester but also one not to overstep because she would set you straight. She would be the person always to make you laugh and was very social. I tend to have these same traits. I'm usually always joking around being funny, even if it's a bad joke. That's just my humanity, my personality.

But in spite of my mother's issues over time, she loved her children to the best of her ability, according to her family and though I regret to say she lost her battle with addiction in 2003, every single detail of her life had a purpose. God gave her two awesome gifts, a daughter and a son, Amanda Carter and me, Jeremiah Carter.

My biological mother named me Jeremiah Isaiah Carter. After two years passed, I was later adopted by Roberta Cain and then named Jeremiah Isaiah Askew Cain. Askew is my adoptive mother's maiden name, although divorced, Cain is her married name. She simply gave me both instead of just one last name. Later on, in my late 20s, I removed "Askew" from my name so there wouldn't be any more confusion when handling business or government-related things. Doing so made my life so much easier. So my official name now is Jeremiah Isaiah Cain, simply just 3 biblical names. I was part of God's plan for my adoptive mom's life. After her only son passed, she was led toward raising foster children. My earliest memories in life were of three boys I considered my brothers. They were Hakeem, Rakeem and Antwon.

All I remember is that they were in my life for a short period, and then one day, I never saw them again. They went back to their families. I didn't fully come to know full details about my adoption until my early twenties. My adoptive mom had three biological children. Two girls and one son, Sequeroia (Cora), Sevonne (Nellie) and Andre. She adopted me and a girl who is my other sister, Aleta. Her only son, Andre, passed when he was around

8. She considered me to be her gift which arrived right on time.

Even though my mom described me as her perfect gift, my childhood in Milwaukee, Wisconsin, then transitioning to Memphis, Tennessee, was everything but perfect. As a child, I witnessed many arguments between Aleta and Nellie, with my adoptive mom trying to calm the situation. It always ended up with Aleta yelling, "Y'all are not my real family anyway!"

When we were around eleven and twelve years old, while taking a family trip to the dentist, one argument between my sisters grew more and more intense to the point of revealing that this isn't her real family. In the parking lot of the dentist's office, as I continued to witness their altercation, I began to question certain things about myself. *Why do I have two last names? Where was my father? Did my mother really give birth to me at age 50? Why doesn't she mention her ex husband being my father when she talks about him? Why is my niece older than me, and I'm the younger uncle?* I asked myself all these questions and concluded, *Hmm, I must be adopted, too.* My mother never confirmed or denied anything about my adoptive history, but due to the odd inconsistencies I witnessed as a child, I knew something was off. One day, out of curiosity, I randomly asked my oldest sister, Cora, "Where is my father?" Her response was, "Umm, you should ask your mom. It would be best to ask her."

I never talked about how this made me feel. My life was like a puzzle with missing pieces to it. I never chose to pursue more information about anything early on. I just kept my feelings in. I figured life was going well for me; therefore, I had no room to complain. I had food, clothes and shelter and although not perfect, I was being raised by a great family. I just kept on living like they were my biological family.

My sister, Aleta, who also was adopted, eventually connected with her biological family when she turned eighteen, and mom decided to send her to be with them permanently. Just a few years later, my mother eventually confirmed that I was in fact, adopted. She also told me that she didn't tell me that I was adopted because she didn't want me to share my sister's perspective out of fear that she might lose her only son again or there would be a possibility of any type of resentment or rejection towards her.

I can also recall the night she called me into her bedroom to show me a picture of me in the arms of a caucasian woman. This woman was from Child Protective Services. My mother told me this woman had given her a prophetic word concerning me. She told my mother that I would be gifted with my hands and that God told her to give this child to my mom.

I was told I was an extremely bad child at an early age. I was all over the place. I would think this is a male boy thing in my experience, behavioural problems, as they say. I definitely got the discipline I needed, which is what all children need.

My adoptive mother worked for the IRS and worked as a nurse in the medical field in her earlier years, but she was retired by the time I came around. I only knew the saved, sanctified mother, an ordained pastor, from my earliest memories. I simply remember having church from inside our house. There is no doubt that she took great care of us and made sure we had the necessities. I recall the little Jesus songs she would sing when coming into the living room and the Bible stories we grew up with. Like Daniel in the Lion's den and David/Goliath and Moses parting the Red Sea leading the Israelites out of Egypt. More than anything, the name Jesus was always mentioned more than anything. My mother was a praying woman; she also prayed in the spirit, an unknown language I didn't understand till later on in life. She was always up early before sunrise singing songs and hymns to the Lord. Although I grew up in church, my relationship with the Lord didn't actually start till I was older and got saved. But the Lord was with me throughout the entire journey. God had a plan, and He had His hand on me. The Bible says,

*"For I know the plans I have for you," says the Lord. "They are plans for good and not for disaster, to give you a future and a hope."*

I remember that my mother was pretty good at old-fashioned cooking. If there's anything I remember the most, it's making sure we had a good meal each day.

I literally remember the same meals each week. My mother always cooked, and they rotated every week.

Monday: Spaghetti & Garlic Toast.

Tuesday: Fried Chicken and Mashed Potatoes.

Wednesday: Roast & potatoes with Corn Bread.

Thursday: Meatloaf & Fried potatoes.

Friday: Pork Chops with cabbage and pinto beans.

In between meals, I recall a lot of Microwave Banquet Dinners, pizza rolls, white castles, hot pockets and different new home-cooked meals from time to time. I was a fat kid growing up. I can definitely say I was fed pretty darn good. Although a bit of a loner, it is safe to say I had a good childhood, and although sheltered, it was still a good childhood.

## Chapter 2

# Cracking the Door of Endless Opportunity

Early on, when I was between 1 and 2 years old, I was considered a few months behind schedule in development after each doctor's visit. Things got better with time. I was called a gifted child and placed in a special education program commonly referred to as *"Resource"* by the time I got to second grade. Ironically, I didn't stay in Resource for long because I excelled in every test I was given. So, one day, I tested out of Resource.

During my early teen years, I experienced what I wouldn't have known then but known today as a father wound. Simply put, a father wound is the psychological and emotional pain that a child experiences due to the absence, neglect, or abuse of a father or father figure. The only father I knew was simply my mother. This began to affect me mentally because every learning opportunity always came from a woman's perspective. Even to the point of comments like, "This is what men do." I truly hated this, but I am thankful for single-parent mothers raising boys to the best of their ability.

One day, this drove me to the point of depression and tears, asking myself why I didn't have a father and why I was sheltered. I just remember lying in bed crying deeply and having suicidal thoughts. I simply felt alone, and the root cause being the feeling of abandonment. Although I didn't have a good relationship with God being young, looking back, He walked with me the entire time and had a plan for my life; I was lonely but truly never alone.

I began to seek out a father figure from people of bad influence, mostly boys in the school because it was the only place I had freedom. I remember times I would seek out the attention of gang members. I wanted to be an Avalon Crip. They wore green bandanas. I asked a guy of high rank if I could get C'd down. He said, *"Yeah, you just gotta come to the hood"*. It didn't happen. I was too sheltered to be away after school for something such as a gang initiation, but this was more than likely God protecting me.

Outside of all the peer pressure and bad influence, which I believe a lot of teens go through. I noticed things that I was truly gifted in, like an inherent gift that almost took no effort. I was truly gifted with computers and applications, and as time progressed, I was also gifted with speaking and teaching. It was the gift of creativity that manifested deeply in all these gifts. The Bible says, *"A man's gift maketh room for him, And bringeth him before great men."*

Later on in high school, a recruiter came to draft some people into a two-year technical school. He mentioned a few programs, but the one that stood out to me was the IT (Information Technology) program. This sparked my interest because I was already gifted with computers, and I learned how to type extremely fast.

It was like a light bulb had been switched on in my head. Everyone was using computers, and with every computer, they would need someone to support them. I then said, "I got it". That's what I wanted to do. I wanted to work with computers and build a career in the technology field. God planted this vision for the future in my head and showed me where I was gifted early. I would ride down different parts of Memphis with my sister, Cora, and see huge corporate buildings. I would always say one day, I would work in those big buildings.

After high school, I decided to enroll in the Network and Systems Administration program at ITT Technical Institute. Things were going so smoothly that I had even become an assistant to the teacher. Shortly after, I got a job as a cashier at Sam's club, my first job, making minimum wage. This job only lasted a few weeks because I decided that it was time for me to pursue a career doing what I loved. So, I learned how to create a resume early.

It was pretty basic, with mainly my school information on it, but it worked out in my favor as I applied to different jobs.

I was invited for an interview at the Baptist Memorial Hospital in Memphis for a computer operator position. It was a short-term contract through Teksystems. The position required an associate's degree, and I only had 2-3 months of trade school. But I didn't care about the requirement because I was ambitious and I had faith, so I applied anyway. At age 19, I landed my very first IT job, and I was on my way.

*Chapter 3*

# All Hope is Not Lost, it's about to get Bigger and Better

I went to school in the day and worked the IT job at night. The job was easy for the most part. I would simply monitor the computers and if any problems occurred, I had to contact the systems engineer or systems administrator to fix the problem. After about six months, the contract for my computer operator position ended. So I updated my resume and started applying to several full time jobs. Almost immediately after, I got a call for an interview with SergeMD, a healthcare IT company, and the interview went extremely well. I was pretty confident. A few weeks later, I landed a position in technical support with them supporting healthcare facilities.

It was at sergeMD where I developed most of my technical skills. I enjoyed the organizational culture and the experience I was gaining. It was the setup, imaging, configuring and troubleshooting of all the computers, and I enjoyed every bit, especially the teamwork. There's always someone else to ask for help and always someone who knows more than you do.

My happiness with the company came to an abrupt end when Serge hired new management. Drastic changes were made, and people began to be fired at least once a month.

When it was my turn, I got called to the office. *"Jeremiah, we're going to have to let you go."* Losing my job challenged my faith a great deal because I had no idea how to manage life without a consistent income.

I sent applications everywhere. This next encounter appeared to be more delightful. I was out for a short period, but I was still stressed out. I had bills to pay. I was ambitious, still searching for the next job. All you could hear was the loud clacking sound of my keyboard.

One day, after sending in so many applications, my sister Cora told me to come into the kitchen. I was a bit down and so she began to pray. She is a Christian. She had been saved for over twenty years, and anyone could tell by her fruit. She began to pray heavily and speak in this unknown language. I was reminded that my adoptive mother spoke in an unknown language as well from time to time. It was strange but powerful. It was a prayer of faith. Almost immediately afterwards, I thanked her and began to walk back to my computer. I felt really different. It was like my strength had been renewed.

What was this power? It was the power of God.

As I walked back to my computer, I saw an email come through. I opened it and saw that it was a job offer. I said, *"Thank you, Jesus."* There's power in that name. It just made me lift my head up and think for a minute. I said to myself, *"There's something about these spiritual things. Biblically, there's something about the name Jesus"*. Although raised in a spiritual home, it was these types of encounters that go beyond simply church. As a wise man once told me, *"Get to know God for yourself"*. I continued on with accepting the job offer without too much deep thought but always thought about encounters like this one from time to time.

Soon after, I started my new job. I worked at a major private law firm. Instead of supporting healthcare workers, I was now supporting the computer systems in the legal industry. Supporting lawyers, paralegals and the like. The skills used were the same—just supporting different people—and, I have to add, different attitudes. It was a fun time. We had to set up and troubleshoot the computers and systems in order for them to keep working. We worked as a team and made sure productivity was good.

After a few years of working in technical support, I began to focus on another vision God planted in me for the future. I had a vision after watching a short video on computer hacking. The vision was to work for a 3 letter government agency in cybersecurity. I became fascinated with the military and government agencies in general. This whole high-level, top-level security clearance and the classified realm of things piqued my interest. The government is huge! So many agencies and so many sub-agencies. I researched them; FBI, CIA, DIA, DOJ, DOD, NGA, and the list goes on.

I started applying, and I received an offer to interview with the Defense Intelligence Agency (DIA). This is a national security agency. I was astonished. I did well in the interview, and they moved forward with my application process. It was a lengthy process. Even though I didn't get the position, I ended up at another 3-letter government agency which had a unique purpose. I later learned that sometimes, God will place you where he wants you to be because it's a part of His plan, and it will be in His perfect timing.

Naturally, it's good to network with people on your journey and develop a good reputation as well. You never know who may end up helping on your journey.

One of the students I went to school with actually contacted me about a position in cybersecurity and told me where to send my application. It's funny; all I had was a vision, faith, and a decent technical background and the position actually came to me. It was all a part of God's plan. Getting into the government sector takes time. It was a fast-paced but patient season for me. As a colleague put it, *"It is the concept of 'hurry up and wait'."* And a very important lesson to note is, *"It's not just what you know, it's who you know."* I received the job offer, and I was on my way.

On my first day, I was escorted by my colleague. I walked into the place, and it was basically everyone I went to school with, including instructors. It was like walking into a party with my school family. I didn't need a formal introduction. I already knew everybody, and they knew me. I began to get acclimated to government processes.

I achieved greatness. I considered myself a successful person. I worked hard for two years got my associate's degree with perfect attendance. I worked in the IT field for a few years and got some good experience on my resume. I succeeded in the vision God planted on the inside.

I learned later this whole journey for me has been Biblical. The Bible says,

*"Write the vision, and make it plain upon tables, that he may run that readeth it."*

The vision was written on my heart. And I kept the faith. The Bible also says;

*"Faith is the substance of things hoped for; the evidence of things unseen"*. I had to believe the vision first before I was able to see it. Thank you, Jesus. Once again, I have to say there is power in His name. All this had a purpose.

*"It's not what we can do for ourselves, it's what we can do for our team."* —*John Russell.*

# Chapter 4

# Perfecting Out Gifts

My job was phenomenal. I began to use my gifts and work on high level technical projects. I worked with people who had military backgrounds, are quick-witted and extremely funny. But at the end of all the fun and jokes, we get the job done. We fulfill the mission of the government. I learned one thing about military people; they look out for each other. They don't leave anyone hanging, even in their personal lives. On this job, I had the best managers known to mankind, especially my first one. I mean to the point where I tried to mirror his mentality. He was like a father to me, he didn't know I looked at him in this way. I really wanted to be like him. I tried but failed utterly. Then I tried to combine that with a "Jocko Willinks" mentality, but that, too, didn't work because that's not who I really am. It took them years in the military to develop most of that mentality. But here I was, trying to have a Seal Team 6 and Marines military mentality when each of us needs to be ourselves simply; we're all unique and made exactly how God wants us to be. So I would advise anyone, just be yourself, don't try to be like anyone else. You're perfect and authentic, just the way you are and were created to be.

After working for a year, I decided to help other people learn about computers, so I applied for a job as an instructor at a vocational school, Remington College. I had a two-year degree, which makes me qualified to teach at a two-year vocational school (a hands-on school). I got a call and the interview was with one of the instructors that taught at the school I graduated from. I was 24 years old at the time. I was the youngest Instructor in the school. People calling me by my last name was pretty weird at first, but I got used to it. In my first class, there was a little bit of rejection due to my age. But by the second class, everyone was calling me Mr. Cain because they had come to realize I was able to provide hands-on teaching, and I knew what I was doing. It was like I had to earn their respect. Some students were twice my age, but surprisingly, I was able to teach similar to how they teach in colleges. I taught this way on a whiteboard and then proceeded with hands-on teaching. Teaching was something I learned I was gifted in. There was purpose in these experiences.

I learned that you're never too old to learn and never too young to teach. It helped me to know that it's good to improve on our gifts.

So, things were great and phenomenal in this chapter of my life.

I'm successfully working in Cybersecurity, I am teaching in a school, I do boxing and kickboxing as a form of workout to stay in shape, and everything was great with the family, so I eventually began to date. I met this woman who I became attracted to, my first love. She was a flight attendant, lived out of town and wasn't around most of the time at the beginning. After a short period of time being friends, we got into a relationship. We had a phenomenal time flying and spending a lot of time together. The relationship was long-distance, but we made it work. We would talk about things I was open about and things I hadn't even mentioned to my family or anyone else. I didn't think it was a big deal. I just believed everything happens for a reason, even birth and, in my case, adoption.

She told me she was adopted and that she found her biological family. So, I opened up to her about it and told her, *"I was adopted, too, and I told her I didn't know my biological family."* That was a topic I hadn't talked about before, but it didn't bother me as much when I think about the positive sides of my life growing up being taken care of. It's just something I've always kept in. I also told her, *"Even as an adult, my adoptive family and I have never talked about my adoption."* They believed that I thought they were my real biological family.

21

But here's the thing, there was a purpose in being raised with this family, so there had never been a problem. It was all part of God's plan. She then said that I could actually find them because there are companies that can help you trace your biological family if you were adopted. So I told her maybe I'll look into that. I didn't think about it for some time.

## *Chapter 5*

# A Divine Purpose and Plan is set forth

I finally moved into my apartment (my man cave). I tell you, as a man, there is no greater feeling than when you set out to be on your own. One day, while at home, something piqued my interest/curiosity about my biological family. I felt I had to find them; I felt like there was a pull on my spirit.

I did my research, and I found a company that provided those kinds of services. The Department of Children and Families helped me. I paid the fee and gave them the basic information they required to start the search. After about a week or two, I received a call from them. They informed me that they had found the records regarding my adoption.

The only sad news was that my mother had passed. They sent me the records via email. I went through the document, about 150 pages, of some of my biological mother's past and my past from when I was born till I was adopted at the age of 2. I read through them as if it was a book. It seemed a bit rocky at first, but I read it calmly.

To summarize the adoption records, it was as if they were trying to get a point across. My life began to shift. A shift towards the revelation that there is a divine purpose and plan set forth.

"This child was abandoned"

"This child is behind on development."

"This child has been neglected."

"This child was abandoned"

That was what they made it look like on paper in the natural world. But in the spiritual world, that wasn't the case. Even in situations where there is abandonment naturally, spiritually, God has never abandoned you. The Bible says,

*I will never leave you nor forsake you.*

He is always with you. And has been from the beginning till even now. My life had a purpose so does yours.

I kept reading, and my spirit was extremely calmed. I didn't feel anything. I didn't feel neglected; I didn't feel abandoned at all at the time, but it was quite a bit of information to take in reading about my past. I actually felt relief that I was able to find out about my past, although I felt there was something birthing inside of me. It was like there was a cry for help or something. Like people need to know, if God walked with me through this process, He is also with you. I felt there had to be a reason for this. After I was done reading through it, I felt a pull to just reach out and find them. I began my search. I went on social media and started sending messages to people, telling them who I was. It was one wrong person after the other. This made me almost give up, but I persisted.

I found one person who turned out to be a cousin. I sent her a message and she was so astonished and happy and said she knew exactly who I was. I then got a few friend requests from some people. I gave them my number, and they called. What started out as a one-on-one call became a conference call. I received nothing but love from these people. The comments the majority of them made was, *"You look just like your mother."* I was happy; it was all smiles and laughs. I had found my biological family and connected with them. I felt so fulfilled, it was like a missing piece to a puzzle. The adoption was all part of the God's plan. A lot of the family weren't raised together. There were trying circumstances that may have caused separation, but there is a purpose in everything.

I hadn't told my adoptive family any of this. I was still thinking of how to relay this without making things uncomfortable. I was happy and in good spirits and I didn't want that to change.

I introduced my girlfriend at the time to my adoptive family, and we went out to eat one day with my oldest sister Cora. Everything was going well at the beginning. We had conversations about life, work, flying, etc. Let me remind you my family and I have "never" discussed my adoption and finding my biological family yet. So, at this time, they are still under the impression that I believe they are my biological family. The conversation was awesome, in the beginning, we laughed and talked about everything.

Somewhere along the line, my girlfriend at the time blurted out the words, *"Well, it turns out Jeremiah and I are both adopted,"* and blah, blah, blah (kept talking like one would in a normal conversation).

I don't know if she realized she had opened a door that could never be closed again. I didn't expect the adoption news to be revealed this way. I had to hold my composure in the middle of eating my sushi. With my sister's eyes wide open, I thought a tear was going to drop at this time. The reaction on her face was like (OMG) with her eyes opened real huge, and she kept looking straight. After the meal, everything seemed all fine and dandy, but it definitely wasn't. After eating, we departed with a few laughs and played it off like nothing had happened. But eventually, my sister called, and we had a conversation for the first time regarding my adoption. It was a bit emotional, but I told her I was fine and that I found my biological family on my mother's side. We then planned how to have "the talk" with my adoptive mother.

A few days later, I visited my adoptive mother; I walked to her and asked her if she had a minute to talk. She said yes. I closed the door and we talked. I started by saying, *"So I'm adopted."* She said, *"yeahhhhh"*, slowly and calmly. It felt like it was going to be a History lesson. She leaned back in her chair and told me everything. We talked for some time. It was a great conversation. She told me I was a blessing because she lost her biological son at an early age, and getting foster children was something God led her to do. She is an ordained pastor, and God blessed her by leading her to adopt me. It was all part of the purpose and plan of her life. We don't always understand these things and don't even understand the circumstances, but God is in control of everything, and we just have to trust him.

Don't try to figure out God's plan, no one knows the plans God has from beginning to end. Only He knows, so just trust him.

The Bible says,

*"Yet God has made everything beautiful for its own time. He has planted eternity in the human heart, but even so, people cannot see the whole scope of God's work from beginning to end."*

I truly didn't understand the circumstances, but God knows. She ministered to me one day when my spirit was down a bit. She came to me and said, "God already knew the plan, Jeremiah. He knew His plans for you before you were born." The Bible says,

*"Before I formed thee in the belly, I knew thee; and before thou camest forth out of the womb, I sanctified thee."*

The life lesson of the Prophet Jeremiah can be used as an example to show us that God has a purpose and plan for every child before they are even born. Thus, I would tell anyone, under any trying circumstances, don't abort your child because God will use that child one day. I thank God my biological mother did not abort me. To God be the glory.

## Chapter 6

# Imperfectly Perfect

A few days later, I was invited to a wedding so that was an opportunity to meet my biological family for the first time. I take the trip down there. I was humbly welcomed by aunties, uncles and cousins. It was awesome getting to know we were alike in many ways. For example, we like our cereal crunchy; if we leave it out too long and it gets soggy, we make it again. We were also funny, loved to laugh and have a good time. Another thing I also noticed was that we like our food to be separate and not close to one another's. I fit right in with them because this was my family by blood.

One of my uncles had to introduce me to many new kinds of foods. One day, he asked, "*Why don't you know*

29

*about these foods?"* my answer was, *"I was a sheltered child"*, and they started introducing me to all sorts of good foods I hadn't heard about.

I was a neutral ground person coming into my biological family, not knowing about any problems of the past, the "brokenness". I was focusing on the now and moving forward. I had connected to various members of the family, some of which may have been a little distant from each other, but after a talk with them individually, one day, I received a few calls and texts saying that everyone was on a conference call together. It was a joy seeing how God did that. It was such a blessing. The family and I started getting more acquainted, and we took vacations together, nothing but laughs and a good time.

My spiritual uncle and auntie went to their church and prayed for me, and afterwards, I learned I have a special "calling" on my life, that God had a plan for me. Surprisingly, I learned that what you go through in life, in many cases, is what ministry and people you are called to. Some people have a heavy calling, like pastoring a megachurch, and some people have a smaller calling, such as simply serving others. The Bible says,

*"For the gifts and callings of God come without repentance."*

This spiritual calling was very important and new to me. I began to change spiritually almost immediately. I joined a local church and got *"saved"*.

What does it mean to be *"saved"*?

It simply means to believe in the Lord Jesus; the Bible says,

*"If you openly declare that Jesus is Lord and believe in your heart that God raised him from the dead, you will be saved."*

Once you're saved, your whole life changes. If you're living in sin, the Holy Spirit convicts you of that sin and you no longer desire to sin anymore. You also learn that God had a plan for you from the very beginning, and your life will be structured according to His will. So, I encourage you now to get saved because God loves you.

The church I joined turned out to be an extremely large church, the motto being "one church in two locations". I had to go through the courses before becoming active in anything.

I started working hard by helping in different areas of the ministry. I enjoyed every bit of it. Meeting new people, talking about the Lord, what they've been through, how God brought them all out, and bringing people into the kingdom. It was just awesome doing the work of God and being in the midst of His people.

If there's anything I learned about the Bible and being saved, it is this. Love. The Bible says this,

*"Teacher, which is the most important commandment in the law of Moses?"* Jesus replied, *"You must love the Lord your God with all your heart, all your soul, and all your mind."* This is the first and greatest commandment. A second is equally important: *"Love your neighbor as yourself."* The entire law

and all the demands of the prophets are based on these two commandments.

So, I started learning more about spiritual gifts. I had many divine encounters as I met people and did nice things. I began to do things and I was spiritually led by God to do. One of which is encouraging people. Another was I would give physical gifts; in one case, I gave someone a devotional, which that person and others would confirm and say, "This had to be God".

I began to come close to The Bishop in church, my pastor and after getting close to him, he became like a father to me, the father I never had, unbeknownst to him. I didn't care so much to be near him on Sunday when he preached, but throughout the week, it was a more personal connection. I remember the first time I told him that I believed I was going to be on vacation. He responded, *"Enjoy, have fun son."* Calling me son really made me feel blessed. I never had that before, especially from a man. From then on, I just wanted to be near him all the time.

When it came to family, I had the best of both worlds. I had my adoptive family, my biological family, my work family and now venturing into a new family, the body of Christ. So, I technically found that I have multiple families, so you're never alone on this journey. When it seems there is no blood or natural family. There is always family in the Kingdom, the body of Christ. Even when it seems there's no one, God is always with you, and He knows who and when to send someone into your life. You may be lonely, but you're never alone. This is one reason why it's good to be saved; you will know that God is always with you.

Life was perfect in my head. I was doing well in my career, and I was teaching students at a school. I found my biological family, and I enjoyed being part of both families. I had fun traveling with my girlfriend. I was extremely healthy and in good shape. I had developed a strong relationship with God. Life couldn't be any better than this.

But in the process of enjoying what I considered a perfect life, things began to change because of the journey with God. The journey is not going to be easy; it's a process, and you have to trust Him. The Lord was setting me up for a powerful "testimony". The Bible says,

*"And they overcame him by the blood of the Lamb, and by the word of their testimony."*

Wherever you are in life (Job, Jail, Mental health facility, nursing home, school, a corner, at home, or church), whether life seems perfect or you feel you're at wits end, Put your trust in God; he will see you through. It's easy to trust him when things are going good and "imperfectly perfect", but can you trust Him when things are not going so well?

How? Pray and READ His Word. The Bible says,

*"Trust in the Lord with all thine heart, and lean not unto thine own understanding. In all thy ways acknowledge Him, And he shall direct thy paths."*

*Chapter 7*

# Death and Life Are in the Power of the Tongue

I got home one day after working out at the gym, showered and relaxed for a few minutes. I then decided to go through my adoption records again. I got all the way through them to the end when I saw something strange.

It read, *"Jeremiah has been diagnosed with ADHD."*

I pondered over what I had just read. I had never seen or heard of this term. I didn't know anything about diagnoses. I didn't even know the term *"mental health"* was a thing. As far as I knew, I didn't have any problems mentally. Even if I did, I didn't recognize it.

As a wise man told me *"after"* the crisis when I asked him about mental health, he said these profound words, *"Jeremiah, there's nothing wrong with you."* Then he said, *"Jeremiah, you have a brain and imagination".* He paused, then said, *"Anything else said about you is simply man-made".* This was very encouraging, but God knows the plans.

As far as I knew, I was just gifted. I was gifted with my hands (working in Cybersecurity for the federal government). I was gifted with teaching students at a school. I was healthy and in good shape. I was starting to get to know God more after hearing about this "calling" on my life and getting saved. Everything was perfectly fine. I didn't have any mental health issues as far as I knew. I was fine.

So, what in the world was this diagnosis on paper? What was this unknown condition that I was supposedly diagnosed with? I looked the illness up, and boy, did my life change. Everything turned upside down after this.

The Bible says,

*"As a man thinketh in his heart, so is he."*

In other words, you are what you think.

The Bible also says;

*"Death and life are in the power of the tongue."*

I've heard these scriptures being used on many occasions, especially through motivational speaking, but didn't think deeply about them that it could become a concrete reality. The first time I heard about these scriptures was from the world's greatest motivational speaker, Les Brown and a very practical pastor, Dr Myles Munroe.

There's power in words, which is why the Bible is such a powerful book; it's God's Word. You can speak into existence positive things as well as negative. You can speak blessings and prosperity into your life, but at the same time, you can speak death and curses. I started talking about the condition and all the symptoms. I mean, I just claimed the condition over my life since it's documented on paper. So, I believed it to be true. Everyone experiences forgetting why they walked into the room sometimes, or may have a small hint of impulsivity. I know that people get distracted every once in a while, but I didn't think there was a medical term for it or something such as a mental health diagnosis.

I could literally feel my brain making changes, the neurological connectors altering. I then decided to speak with a few people in my biological family about it, and that was when I learned that mental health issues run in our family (something about it being a generational thing). My biological family told me stories about different family members over time having major mental health issues. What it appears to be, I had accepted the condition as a permanent truth in my head. Lo and behold, it's like I actually started forcing the symptoms on myself even though I had never experienced issues before. I would say repeatedly, "I have ADHD. It was just at first some instances where I would experience some minor symptoms, but nothing major that could actually affect my well-being until later.

I had an encounter while teaching at school, and I made the decision that it was going to be my last time teaching. I stopped by the director's office one day and noticed he was reading the Bible. I didn't think much of it, but I let him finish. I went back to my classroom and finished up my final lecture. After the students were dismissed, he came into my classroom and sat down to give me a review. He told me that everything was perfect and gave me some advice on one small piece of teaching for the students that could help, which was to stay focused on a particular subject. I told him that I might struggle with that just a little because I found that I have "ADHD".

He looked like he heard that I lost a million dollars by accident based on his reaction. He simply looked up at me real slowly and stared at me like I was a bit crazy, with his eyes opened real huge. Then, he slowly went back to what he was doing. For some reason, I couldn't get that reaction out of my head. I felt naive and indifferent. Why did he give me that reaction when I mentioned I have "ADHD" and he just finished reading the Bible? This memory would come to mind from time to time.

So shortly after, I go to Texas to see my girlfriend, and I informed her I had ADHD and that I needed help, and quick. Not knowing who else to go see with my problems, my girlfriend and I drove to a neurologist. With my limited knowledge, all I knew was that it was a brain issue. The neurologist ran a number of scans on me and said he saw nothing wrong. He said, "With the problem and symptoms you're describing, you need to go see a psychiatrist." I get back to Memphis and I make plans to go see a psychiatrist. I learn that there are 100s of psychiatrists available. I ask, "Why are there so many psychiatrists out there?" This was a whole new world to me.

So I went to see a psychiatrist, told him I have this condition, and then showed him my adoption records. He decided to do a test on my brain which was called a Neba test. I had to stare at a dot in the wall for about 10 minutes while the test was being done with wires attached to my head.

After reading what was on my record and running this neba test, he said, "*Yes, you do have it*". He stated, "*If you were diagnosed at a young age, then you would still have it through adulthood*". Also, he is one of the most highly reviewed and well-known Psychiatrists in Memphis!

After asking me a few questions about my health history, he prepared to put me on stimulant medication. I never struggled with major anxiety before and never needed medication for anything. Almost every day, this claim of ADHD would push my anxiety to the max. I would go everywhere repeating the words to myself, "I have ADHD". This was one unique journey for the books. It was anxiety all the way to the psychiatrist because this condition apparently had to be fixed with meds.

I was very anxious, and all I could think was *I need this fix now*. I was given my first dose. They started with a small dose. This was new to me. I learned they work with patients in phases until they find the right medication for each individual person's mental health diagnosis. After receiving my first sample prescription, which was called "*Concerta*". I went to Walgreens to fill it. I took the pill with water, and then got in my car. Impulsive and distracted by everything, I fumbled for my keys and, when I found them, drove off.

(After driving for a few minutes, I could feel my brain changing. It was like I was at a stoplight; I closed my eyes and opened them slowly…. And the PARTY BEGAN!!!! It was working! )

I felt powerful and invincible beyond measure. I could see clearly; it was like a tunnel vision, a deep state. I understood things faster. I then turned on the radio. It was "*club time*". It was a party with no limits. I wanted to learn how everything works. I go to Barnes & Noble and pick up a book titled "*How Everything Works*". I didn't realize this fix would come with superpowers in my head, of course.

The medication had me thinking I could really be anything; a doctor, lawyer, mathematician, physicist, chemist, historian, politician, you name it. Yesss, I was going to master them all. When I got home, I created a huge amount of documents on my computer for almost every career available. The goal was to pick a career and just study as much as possible about it. I was going to be a jack of all trades and the master of all. There was purpose in this experience, too. Let me explain this purpose and lesson before I get back to my crisis. This was an attempt to get me off course, and I'm sure it happens to a lot of people as well. The Bible says,

*"All things are lawful unto me, but not all things are expedient."*

In one interpretation, this means that out of the hundreds of career options available, you are permitted to choose anyone you want, but not all these options will truly benefit you (they are not part of the divine purpose and plan that was predestined for your life), and it definitely wasn't for me.

Lo and behold, after a few hours, I started losing all my power, all my knowledge, all the logic, all the precision, all the focus. The supernatural, deep state, just gone. My fix was fleeting. I panicked, I became impulsive, and my anxiety pressed to the max.

When the medication wore off, this is when I really started to experience the full effects and symptoms of ADHD. It became a reality *"after"* the stimulant medication.

Looking at the time, the psychiatrists would be closed. I had to wait till the next day, so I decided to try and get some sleep. I was full of anxiety, I felt neglected, full of fear, I felt all alone, I felt abandoned.

I then had a horrific encounter, I saw a human image appear while awake, and it scared the living crap out of me. I nearly jumped out of my skin. Although these meds supposedly came with superpowers in my head, they also came with side effects. I did some research and ran across the term Schizophrenia. Unfortunately, I said, *"I must have this condition too."*

I woke up the next morning with only one task in mind; go straight to that psychiatrist and tell him what happened. He then switched me to a new medication called Vyvanse. I tested this medication and told him it worked, so I received a 30-day dose. I was excited. I had finally got my fix back, my power, and my secret pill.

I would take the medication, and within fifteen minutes, I would close my eyes and open them very slowly... yessss, the superpowers awakening; the power beyond measure, the eagle eye vision, logic like never before. Limitless, powerful and unstoppable again. I signed back up to college and everything. I would take the meds and just study, study, and ace everything. I would go out with people, and I would just release knowledge from all the studying. Yes, give me a seat at the table of the high-IQ people, the so-called intellectuals.

But wait, I decreed and declared a mental health disorder at first. So, every symptom manifested in the beginning after my first dose; I was slow to speak, words and comments were completely short and vague, I was easily distracted by my surroundings, I was impulsive and forgetful, full of anxiety around everyone. They would start to talk, and I could not keep up or engage in the conversation. But I would find the right time to pull out my fix, slip the pill into my mouth and wash it down with water. I would put the drink down with a smirk, gritting my teeth and laughing profusely on the inside. Then I would wait until I started to feel it… yesss. I would close my eyes and begin to open them very slowly as the meds take effect. They saw what true intellectualism was after I dropped knowledge from all the studying I had done.

My hero, Albert Einstein, once said, *"I want to know God's thoughts mathematically."* And he was able to solve equations about the universe in a way that the average person couldn't comprehend. It was a rumor that he might've had ADHD, but in actuality, I believe he was just more than gifted. He said he wanted an equation that would calculate all the physical laws of the universe. But the greatest physicist eventually died with this equation unsolved. With my fix, the meds, I got you, Al, I'll finish what you started. This was all in my head, of course.

Just like Einstein would walk around when it's quiet, and he was alone to work on solving an unimaginable equation. I began to do the same eventually … but solving the equation I was pondering in my head was more like a "Tug of War" between things in this natural world vs. things in the spiritual world.

## Chapter 8

# Going Through the Furnace

It was the weekend, and I had an encounter with the Lord. On Sunday, there I was in the service, listening to the Word by my pastor, or rather personally, my spiritual father. For some reason, I couldn't focus on the Word. I learned quickly that, in this case, your adversary (the devil) does not want you to hear the Word or get the Word in you because there is power in the Word. A power that's been here since the beginning. The Bible says,

*"Through faith, we understand that the worlds were framed by the word of God so that things which are seen were not made of things which do appear."*

I left in the middle of the sermon to take a break. As I was walking in the hallway, this minister walked up to me like he knew me already or could see something on me spiritually. He asked me, *"Are you alright? You're walking like you can't focus."* My response was, *"Yeah, I've got ADHD, so I can't focus well in there".* He got angry, almost like he wanted to attack me. He said with authority, *"You don't have ADHD! You have the power of the Holy Spirit",* I remembered the reaction from the director of the school I taught at. I was stunned, ready to argue with him, but I didn't because I respected the minister.

The argument was him speaking the Word and the Holy Spirit vs me speaking mental health and a diagnosis. I really had to scratch my head and ponder that. But I simply replied to him, *"Ok, thanks."* And kept walking. What he said would randomly come to my remembrance every so often pretty heavy, along with other similar encounters. As I sought God more and drew closer to Him, the enemy would also draw nigh to try and get me off course. But God knows the plans.

Upon getting home, I had another encounter that blew my mind. I began to study mental health issues and ran across what was known as the DSM-5. It was this document that had a standard classification of mental disorders, which is used by mental health professionals in the United States. Everything mental health related was all standardized into this document. I ordered the document, and it was like I had been pulled into a deep pit of captivity. The document had about 1000 pages with hundreds of mental health disorders! I guess these answers my earlier question of why there are so many psychiatrists out there.

My reaction!

*You have got to be freaking kidding me; what in the world did I just discover or uncover. I cannot unsee what I see. Are people throughout the world in bondage to all these things, to all these disorders? I myself was put in bondage, in captivity, and as far as I could see, a big percentage of the world is also in bondage and held captive and don't know there is freedom. Who can help free these people?*

*I only have one word to answer this question. The answer is "Jesus".*

The Bible says,

*"And he came to Nazareth, where he had been brought up: and, as his custom was, he went into the synagogue on the sabbath day and stood up to read. And there was delivered unto him the book of the prophet Esaias. And when he had opened the book, he found the place where it was written."*

*Jesus said;*

*"The Spirit of the Lord is upon me Because he hath anointed me to preach the gospel to the poor; He hath sent me to heal the brokenhearted, to preach deliverance to the captives, And recovering of sight to the blind, To set at liberty them that are bruised, To preach the acceptable year of the Lord."*

This prophecy was referring to the one who would come and save the world, deliver people and set people free from a multitude of things, Jesus Christ.

Based on personal experience, mental health is very real. But you can overcome anything, with the power of Jesus Christ spiritually and also things naturally. You have to trust God's process for you. You also have to do what works for you because not everybody is a believer; everything is a process, even people who are not spiritual, and we have to respect their boundaries and their beliefs. This isn't to convert anyone but to give a living testimony of someone who is a Christian. I was being pulled into what I call "the system", a fiery furnace of hell. This reminds me of the 3 Hebrew boys in the fiery furnace. There was a 4th man in the fire, "Jesus", walking with them. For me, it was like a tug of war. It's like the enemy had thrown his rope on me and was winning, reeling me in, and pulling me into the fire, but thank God for Jesus, walking with me through the furnace.

I took a few days off work, testing out the medication I was given. After a few days, I began to experience the side effects. There were times I wouldn't eat. I would be too focused when they are in effect. After the meds wore off, one horrible side effect was that I would start binge eating. Would you believe "binge eating" is actually a disorder? I was astonished; any fast food place I saw, I ate till I was about to explode. I went back to the psychiatrist and told him about the problem. He decided to switch me to a different medication.

This time, it was a term I have ran across, but never gave it a second thought. I was given the medication

"Adderall". Yes! All my powers were back again with less side effects.

My new fix. I said to myself, *"This is the "permanent" solution to this "permanent" diagnoses."* I was set for life as long as I had my fix! The stimulant meds.

So, I returned to my awesome job and updated my boss. He was extremely helpful, along with other colleagues. He said I could take the time off needed to work out the medication phases and keep him posted because I found that I wasn't the only one who struggled with mental health. He was very knowledgeable about mental health issues and so he was of great assistance. It got to a point where I was stable on the medication. I wasn't abusing it. I made sure to follow the schedule and other guidelines. Eventually, I became tolerant, and I was actually stable for an extended period of time.

Everything was going well at this point; I became even more tech-savvy on the job while on medication. I was writing PowerShell scripts, troubleshooting client-side and server-side issues, and then network, VLAN and firewall issues. I was configuring and setting up virtual networks. I was programming applications and learning the different operating systems. I was learning the cyber threat and cyber intelligence mitigation strategies. Not to mention, the quickness of my typing skills made me a mad dog behind the keyboard. Yes, everything became technical.

*"To me, on medication, I was like a technical god, in my head, of course."*

I then began to mention mental health on the job. I was absolutely astonished at the answers I received. A portion of my co-workers told me how they have a mental health disorder or their children are as well and how they were also on medication. This may have been a cultural thing, but I was ashamed for anyone to know I had a diagnosis, took medication or even had a psychiatrist. But my colleagues were pretty open about their mental health. I was relieved to know that I wasn't alone in this. There's a plethora of technology and engineering-savvy professionals in the world who are diagnosed and medicated, and after further research, many in various fields are diagnosed and medicated. And the funny thing is, they learned what works for them. You wouldn't know they are diagnosed with anything because they go about their daily lives and surprisingly look normal. All you would see is how smart and unique they are, and for some, peculiar. And as I said before, that is what works for them.

One of my close coworkers was the first to tell me you have to find out what works for you because he isn't really spiritual. It took him about two years to get stable with meds, and that is what works for him and has worked for years now. He takes his meds every morning and has found a way to structure his life normally, so that is what worked for him, and he is one of the smartest tech-savvy persons I know. I said in my head, if God did it for him this way, he can do it for me and anyone else too. So, if you've found what works for you, keep doing it.

For my process, simply put, I had to *"Trust the Process."* It took getting to know God for myself and trusting His process.

I was trying to manage life. My fix had stopped working, which helped me to focus (I got distracted, and my short-term memory kept getting distorted). There were times when I became hyperactive and talked too much or too fast, and there were times when I couldn't think enough to say something. I would have conversations with people and not understand what they were saying or remember what they said. After each month, the medication became less effective, and so my dose was increased. It appeared to be a recurring thing. The medication would become less effective and they would just keep increasing the dose. I then thought, I'm going to crash if I keep this up, and I'm sure I'm not the first to realize this. I thought, But there has to be a way out!

*Am I stuck in this revolving world of bondage to this diagnoses and stimulant medications?*

*Chapter 9*

# God's Plan

I later learned about the term *bipolar* after researching mental health issues, and my coworker mentioned that he was bipolar and that he was on medication for it. I began to look up forums and it opened my eyes even more. It appears that thousands of people who are diagnosed come together to talk about their journey on these forums. From professionals in the corporate world of various fields to, unfortunately, drug dealers. It was between people who were really struggling, like me and who were just buying and selling the drugs for the money and what I call the supernatural high, but the reality is, it is temporary.

Sadly, I said to myself, *"Maybe I have this too."* I asked my biological family about it, and they confirmed it was a major one that people in the family have struggled with. I claimed the diagnosis and began to speak it over my life, the same as I did with ADHD. Consequently, with changing to a different version of my medication, from extended release to immediate release, because the medication would become less effective, I began to experience some of the symptoms (highs and lows on mood) around the time my psychiatrist switched me to this variation. Somehow, I was always off, in addition to my current struggles. This was very tricky, to be honest. I would be happy for a period of time, and depressed the next minute. I would be happy and then the smallest thing could make me snap with major aggression(this is not who I am personally, I wouldn't harm a fly). Then, there was the impulsive spending. I couldn't control myself. I just had to have whatever I laid my eyes on. It was like a gun was pointed to my head with making a decision to buy something. On top of that, I started having trouble sleeping. It was probably due to the medication. I went back to see the psychiatrist and told him about these new developments. After telling him the symptoms, I was diagnosed with insomnia. In addition to the stimulant, I was put on medication to help me sleep.

I thought about the whole mental health thing, and then I thought about the "calling" and that argument from the minister at my church about the Holy Spirit. Reading the Bible was heavy on my spirit around the time, so one day, after work, I decided to get into it for myself. As a wise man once told me, *"Get to know God for yourself."*

It was a Friday, and my meds had worn off. So I thought to myself, "Let me take one more dose and just read & focus on the Bible and learn more about this whole calling on my life." So, I took the meds and opened the Bible. I vaguely remember what exactly, but I was back and forth throughout the Word. After a few minutes, my fix kicked in, and my focus increased. My intellect heightened quickly. I was receiving so much of the word in my spirit that the whole presence, my whole environment, felt different; it was the medication, of course.

Learning so much... so much revelation from reading.

I even began to listen to Dr. Myles Munroe's sermons (very practical teaching). I went on the listen to sermons about the Holy Spirit. I do vividly recall him stating in one of his sermons that they tried to diagnose his son with "ADHD", and his response was *"No, there's nothing wrong with him".* They did more evaluations and he stated that his son was simply just smarter than the person teaching him.

But while sitting there Scratching my head listening to the sermons and the Bible in front of me, I picked up the medication bottle I had and just looked at it, puzzled. I took the pill out and just looked at it closely. Something strange was going on, and it was like I was about to uncover something.

So then I looked again from an outside looking perspective, the stimulant medication bottle (mental health) on my left hand. Then, the power of God's Word on my right hand. The DSM-5(Mental health diagnoses) is 700+ pages on the left, and God's Word (The Bible) 66 books on the right. Then, financially, I look at the whole pharmaceutical industry, and it's a billion dollar industry. *"There's something here",* I said in my head. I'm going to figure this out, it became my true passion. It became like a Tug of war between conflicting things at this time.

The big question in my head became this. *Is this a life of mental health disorders, or is this part of "God's Plan?"*

I sat back and thought for a minute then I returned to reading the Bible. So much revelation at once. I was getting filled with more knowledge than I know I could contain at once.

After some time of being stuck in focus mode in the Bible, I had to take a break; I really enjoyed the knowledge I received, but as an elder once told me, when it comes to the Word. *"Take your time."*

I went back to the psychiatrist and explained how the medication eventually kept becoming less effective. He then switched me to a medication called Adzenys.

I was going through such a hard time trying to manage my life, living on my own, with bills to pay, church, family, and work. I had fallouts with church members, coworkers and family on both sides. I went from being the person every loved to the person everyone began to hate and think I was crazy, and some no longer wanted to be associated. I was no longer being used by God with gifts and encouragement in the church. Everything was falling apart, and I was losing track of time.

Things were getting so bad staying alone in my apartment wasn't safe for me. I moved back home with my family.

I would wake up and struggle with what task to start first. Should I eat breakfast first? Shower first or clean up first? I would spend about 30 minutes still trying to make a decision. I would finally get myself together and come to work. My situation got worse. This next offer appears to be a blessing and a curse at the same time.

## Chapter 10

# Keeping the Faith

One day, at work, while I struggled to focus on the task at hand, I received a call for a job offer from my manager.

He offered me a new position, which came with a promotion. He didn't know the full extent of my struggles at the time. I accepted the offer without much thought. I later came to the realization that accepting the offer was a big mistake, but remember, *"Everything has a purpose."*

The position was one of the most high level technical and sensitive positions to have. It was a position that made decisions that affect the entire internet infrastructure on a national level. Thank God most of the systems and servers ran on their own for the most part. And I also had my other colleague available the whole time. The team lead went on vacation for one month and that was the toughest month in my position. I struggled to keep up after my medication stopped working. This stuff was deeply technical;

So I tried it anyway. I tried to motivate myself to do it but it was an utmost failure. I didn't have the confidence to say that I couldn't manage this type of position when I had the chance. I hoped my meds would start working so I would catch up and get up to speed because that was who I am; an ambitious person, but I became dependent on the meds to function. After so many failures on the technical side, I went into a deep suicidal state. On most days, I would go into different areas of the data center to get away from people.

Although medication can be temporary—depending on what works for you—your job needs to have things in place to accommodate you. My boss provided me with all the things I needed once he found out what was going on. He worked with me throughout my whole mental health crisis. He was the best.

At the time, my only problem was that I was struggling so bad with all the symptoms to the extent that I just wanted to escape. I said to myself, *"Let me just leave home, leave my job, leave family, church, everything."* So I sat down and asked myself, *"How can I escape in the data center?"* I began to hear voices in my head.

A voice said softly, *"Join the military; this will help you escape."*

I thought that was God, but it wasn't. I remembered there was something called a spiritual calling; this gave me a little relief. I informed my boss that I was leaving for the military. He was very supportive, but he didn't think it was a good idea (this was God), considering everything I had going on. He believed I needed to stay. Another thing I learned from this experience is that God will use people in different ways to help you. He will always send a helper. God used my boss in a miraculous way. So, trying to join the military was obviously not a good idea, but I just wanted to escape.

Escape the meds, the diagnoses, escape rejection, escape the feeling of abandonment, escape everything. I felt all alone in this. I was actually lonely, but never alone. God was always with me.

So, the weekend came, and I ended up going to see my biological family before making my escape from this bondage. They didn't know what was going on, and I completely forgot and left my meds at home. I didn't tell them what I was going through. I think we've all been here before… I was mad at God. I asked Him why I was still stuck like this. *"Everything was fine before you got involved,"* I said. I almost gave up my faith. I said to Him, *"God, prove yourself."* I kept on ranting. I needed to vent. I continued, *"There's no way you exist. I can't see you; I can't feel you… you don't exist."* I asked myself, *"How can I believe that someone who died was raised from the dead after 3 days? How can someone walk on water, heal the blind, the lame, lepers, and cure all diseases?" Who could believe this?* The whole 5 hours' drive was just me ranting to God. So I ended with this, "*God, if you're real, prove it, prove yourself!*" At that point, I was hanging on to the little faith I had. There were instances where giving up felt like the only option, but something about the "*calling*" and the encounters, like when my sister prayed for me and I received that job offer would come back to my remembrance.

On the walk with God, He is always with you; He is omnipresent. You sometimes believe you have been tricked and simply don't understand why. At times, you lose your faith in Him. And sometimes, too, you feel you've been lied to about everything. He works in different ways, through nature, through people and through trying circumstances, the dark times. Everybody's journey with God is unique. Even when it seems like he absent or quiet, he's always there, walking with you on the journey.

*Chapter 11*

# The BREAKING POINT PART 1: Divine Encounter & The Escape

I paid my biological family a visit; I still had plans to escape later. I had a major breakthrough! A divine encounter with one of my uncles, who was very spiritual, an assistant pastor. I talked with him via phone. What started out as a normal conversation with my uncle became a mental health topic. That was the divine encounter I was asking God for; that restored my faith tremendously.

I mentioned mental health being something that was "permanent", and with my limited knowledge, I thought you had to live with it forever. He revealed something to me that made my brain go into a different state. It seemed like everything was beginning to reverse like the order was reversed. It was that same feeling I had when I first spoke these terms over my life when I saw the diagnoses on paper. I felt the power of God *restoring* me, altering the chemicals in my head.

My spiritual uncle said,

"*Mental health issues don't have to be permanent.*" He continued to say that, in the spiritual world, in many cases, they are generational curses. "*These curses (disorders) as it relates to the brain can be broken.*"

He then said, "*I was able to break the curse off my family and generation earlier in my life through prayer and the Word.*" This wasn't physical, it was spiritual. For some, it's a process for the plan that God has for them.

I was astonished hearing this. I couldn't stop thinking about this. After getting off the phone, I sat up with my back on my pillow. I began to seek God more. My faith was restored greatly. Something deeply powerful was birthing inside of me. I said to myself, "*I need to break these curses off; this condition doesn't have to be permanent.*" But it's a process to know God's plan, and nothing happens overnight. It's just like losing weight; it's a process. It's just like those who are diabetic and have to take medication for it. The same even occurs for mental health, I learned as I matured. So, you have to trust God's process. I was now regaining my ambition but in a completely different direction. I began to think about my *"purpose"*. *What is my purpose?* The Bible says,

*"You can make many plans, but the Lord's purpose will prevail."*

… but then, the attacks become stronger!

Another one of my uncles invited me to his church to help with some community work. Upon arriving at the church, I told them I'll be inside shortly. I go park the car. Then, all of a sudden, I was starting to lose my mind. Surely, my family didn't know all that I was going through.

I was starting to clean up the neighborhood from any trash in people's personal yards. It was a neighborhood with a high rate of crime and gang affiliation. After cleaning up, I took off some of my clothes and left different pieces of my clothes in different areas of the streets. I began to become a monster, a raging animal in my mind, first like a lion protecting his territory. Then, I began digging like a dog, trying to bury his bone in the ground. It was crazy, I then became like a man who could not be tamed, then I passed out briefly. After coming back from the trance, I realized everything was blurry. I heard my uncles screaming my name and holding me, and everything came back to normal. I was embarrassed and didn't know how to explain what happened, so I didn't say anything.

In the car with my Auntie, as they were driving me back to their house, the only thing I remember is stating that I'm sorry about all this and mentioning my mental health struggles.

They called my adoptive family and told them about what had happened. They brought my psychiatric medication with them. They were very supportive. I learned that God won't put more on you than you can bear. Because God is faithful. The Bible says,

*"There hath no temptation taken you but such as is common to man: but God is faithful, who will not suffer you to be tempted above that ye are able; but will with the temptation also make a way to escape, that ye may be able to bear it."*

I was brought safely back home with my adoptive family.

Although I held on to my faith, I was very suicidal. I had a few brothers and sisters in the church who came to my aid. God would send them at the "right time". I received many calls during this time through which they ministered a word to keep me alive. Ministers and elders would call. Then, one day I texted my pastor everything that was going on. He texted me back one scripture. He texted;

*"If the Son therefore shall make you free, ye shall be free indeed."*

He was referring to Jesus.

Then, that night, I thought about Jesus and began to seek his face. It was a moment of peace that surpassed all understanding. In the physical world, I was an adult. But in the spiritual world, "I was a babe" growing up. I wept from all the pain of this process and just would talk to Jesus. The Bible says,

*"Come to me, all of you who are weary and carry heavy burdens, and I will give you rest. Take my yoke upon you. Let me teach you because I am humble and gentle at heart, and you will find rest for your souls."*

Each day, I felt stronger. I could feel myself growing and becoming stronger each day, even though I was still going through the furnace of hell. I went to work, and people saw my struggles. I was still in bondage, but I was getting God's "Word" in me. I kept the word in my heart to get me through the persecution. As a follower of Him, it just felt like I was suffering just like He suffered. The Bible says,

*"Therefore I take pleasure in infirmities, in reproaches, in necessities, in persecutions, in distresses for Christ's sake: for when I am weak, then am I strong."*

I believed I was at wits end, not even including the fact that I hear voices, the enemy talking each day that I won't make it. I'm weak then I'm stronger each day. I then again felt alone and abandoned; I felt hopeless, in bondage, captivity, in prison. I was in Hell on earth, but with the word in me, I felt strong within. This was conflicting; it was war. The DSM-5/mental health/psychiatry on one side, God's Word/my calling on the other. I chose to begin standing firm on the Word of God in the midst of this thorn in my flesh I so badly wanted to be taken away. The Bible says,

*"Even though I have received such wonderful revelations from God. So, to keep me from becoming proud, I was given a thorn in my flesh, a messenger from Satan to torment me and keep me from becoming proud. Three different times, I begged the Lord to take it away. Each time, he said, My grace is all you need. My power works best in weakness." So now I am glad to boast about my weaknesses so that the power of Christ can work through me."*

This torment was the thorn in my flesh, but I thank God for His grace.

The enemy can only go so far, especially when you are walking with God. Remember his servant Job; God allowed all the bad things to befall him and then multiplied him in the end. No matter what you go through, trust God. So, I told myself I wanted to be free from this. I needed to free myself from all this. I remembered, my uncle spiritual told me that this was a generational curse, but it could be broken, that restored my faith tremendously. But you have to trust God's plan for your life; it's never what plan you conjure up.

I took the DSM-5 document, put it in a crate, and took it to my church and left a note and said pray these curses off of me. I got in my car and just drove away as far as I could. I ended up in Texas, in an unknown place. I had left work without saying a word to anyone about where I was going I was going through. I was absent from work for an extended period of time. But I had favor, grace and mercy, and God was in control. God used my manager in a miraculous way. My manager was an ex-marine in the military, so he was able to vouch for me, which helped me keep my job (He ended up getting a hold of my sister Cora via phone). He said, *"I would never fire Jeremiah; I know his heart. He's been faithful for the years he's been here. He was fine, and until he discovered something about mental health and these other issues,"* He went out of his way to help me.

Eventually, I was considered missing. He had contacts in the military and on the job, which helped him when he pondered on sending out an alert and have special agents come look for me. While in Texas, I was hearing the voices again directing me to turn left and right on certain streets till I got to this destination. When I got there, military was based at the place and approached me and said, *"You're in one of the most dangerous parts of Texas, let's get you away from here."* They went to their posts, secured the area and made sure I was protected and could not be harmed until I drove away safely.

Boy, I felt so secured. I felt Gods presence all around me. God was protecting me, and he had plans to bring me out of this. I simply just wanted to escape it all.

*Chapter 12*

# The BREAKING POINT PART 2: Mental Health Facilities

I got back in my car and drove off. While driving, I received a call from my pastor in Memphis, and he spoke some wisdom into me and told me I needed to go back home. I didn't listen to him and kept on driving. I didn't exactly know where I was going, but again, I started following this voice that was guiding me. I ended up at a bay where people went if they were taking a cruise. I stayed up in my car all night. The parking lot was empty. I started losing my mind again, and I didn't have any meds with me. It was worse on this encounter.

From visions to unwanted thoughts and various symptoms, I became unstable. I became once again, a monster in that parking lot. I no longer had control of my mind. I was acting out different animals and insects and movie scenes. First, I crawled around like a spider. Then the lion again, then the grasshopper, and then the gorilla. Then it was Zeus, then Storm, from X-men. At 7am, cars began showing up. People got out of their cars and stared at me. Some pulled out their cameras and recorded me. More cars started showing up and people kept pointing fingers at me. Then, a couple of guys approached me slowly and asked, *"Are you alright?"* The last thing I remember was me jumping toward them as if I was Wolverine. Some of them laughed at this. "*He thinks he's wolverine,*" they said. I even had the three pencils between my knuckles.

Someone called the police, and they showed up. They approached me kindly, put me in handcuffs and put me in the police car. I was thinking, *God, am I really going to go to jail?* While in the car, everything seemed to be going in slow motion. The police ended up taking me to this huge building that had Methodist Richardson Hospital written at the front. The policemen took me out of the car and walked me in. They checked me into the place and then removed my handcuffs. The policemen sat with me for a while until a nurse came to get me, and then they left.

They took my belongings, gave me new clothes to put on and took me to this vacant room. A guy came in and asked me some questions. Once he was done, he led me to another room that looked more like a hospital room. After taking a look around, the place seemed to be a hospital, but very accommodating. The nurse came in to take my vitals and checked my temperature and blood pressure. Everything checked out fine. They then took me to another room where there was a small TV and a remote control. After being there for a few hours, they brought me lunch and snacks. I was very comfortable. I felt this was the best thing that could happen to me. Who knew I would find so much comfort in a hospital. I got another visit from a nurse who told me I was being taken to the second floor and, so I should follow her. Once we got to the second floor, I saw other patients who were also there to get treated.

That floor looked completely different from the first floor. They checked me in and walked me to my room. Some of the patients looked at me hungrily like I was some kind of meat; it was as if they hadn't eaten in days. There were two beds and a cabinet in the room I was taken to.

I walked among people who were acting just like I did at the bay. I was calm, but I felt this was a snippet of lives of many people who were also in bondage. Every conversation I had with people was what came down to this; mental health disorders. My eyes were opened to what type of facility this was at this time; it was a mental health facility, and this was all new to me. This realization made me laugh whenever I talked to some of them. Some of the patients were millionaires. I thought to myself, "Wow! A disorder doesn't care how much money you have or make." During my time there, I ask for a Bible. I found out that they kept bibles in every mental health facility. I was at peace once again, even though I felt I was in prison, but God was with me.

I had confidence that everything was going to be okay. It was funny and even strange that after reading parts of the  Bible, it felt like my mind was completely healed and was clear. And this is no exaggeration; it felt like I was the smartest person in there. Taking my time with so much in the Bible, my faith was getting fully restored. I was there for a few days until my family found out where I was and planned to come to get me. It was my sister Cora and my adoptive mom. We are a praying family, so they prayed and ministered to me while there, keeping me encouraged. I passed every psychological test their psychiatrists gave me). I would be called to speak with a psychiatrist in the midst of reading the Bible, and after some evaluations, they couldn't find anything wrong with me. Some couldn't quite figure out why I was there. But based on the police report, they diagnosed me with *"Bipolar II"* and *"Paranoid Schizophrenia"*.

My sister gets in touch with one of her close friends who lives in Texas. They come and get me from the hospital once they find out I have a release date. I get put in a hotel, and I feel freedom, I feel God *restoring* me.

My sister and my mom come to get me and we go get a bite to eat.

The trip back home was me meditating on the Lord. We come back home, and I begin to have more issues mentally. The battle isn't over. My reality mixed, and I begin to think people are out to kill me. I was always looking out the window to the left and to the right. I would hear the sound of motorcycles, and it would drive my anxiety to the max, thinking they were closing in on me. I get in my car again and drive with no destination in mind. I drive all the way to MS with no money until my car runs out of gas in the middle of a two-way street. I just let my seat back, and I fall asleep.

About an hour later, a cop knocks on my window and wakes me up. He asks me if I was ok; I would begin to speak in code because I would always think the powers to be (the government) was listening and tracking me. He said with a confused look, *"Would you like to go to the hospital?"* I said, *"sure".* So, they take me to a nearby hospital, and I feel safe/secure. My sister Cora finds out where I am again and comes to get me and they bring me back home.

They take me immediately to a place called Lakeside, a mental health facility in Memphis. I've heard of this place but never knew what it was exactly like to be here or for what purpose. They check me in; this place isn't like Texas; it's more like… Memphis, of course. I was used to how things worked in Texas, but just a different environment of people; you could easily tell the socioeconomic difference between here and Texas.

I stay to myself; I asked for the same request in this place, a Bible. They carried only the New Testament, this worked just fine, and I ask if they have paper or a notebook to write on, and they provided that. Day after day, I just read the Bible from morning till night. The peace was unimaginable; it was like being in the Garden of Eden.

I speak with psychiatrists there, and they would scratch their head. I passed all the tests just fine in a calm manner, they couldn't seem to figure out why I was there. It's like they would sigh and say something along the line of getting me out of here soon.

God planted another vision in me, which was becoming an author and writing a book during a peaceful time. I feel God planted that seed in me to come to pass in His appointed season, which you are now reading about. This was a part of God's plan, a part of God revealing part of my "purpose" here on this earth to help people who struggle like I have. And in this, to give Him all the Glory. But I still had to *"Trust the Process."*

My sister and mother came to check on me while there. I also had a few church members who always prayed and kept in contact with me throughout the process.

When I was released to go, I was picked up by my sister. One of the mental health technicians pulled my sister to the side and told her how peaceful and humbled I was there. Like when they called *"Smoke Break",* everyone would run like it's a million dollars on the floor to go smoke. I would be the only one to stay in a corner and just read the Bible. I didn't understand why so many people rush to a cancer-infested drug such as a cigarette when your healing can simply come from God through the power of His Word. All you need on this journey is a Bible; it's all about Him and your journey with Him.

They release me. I leave this place, and my mindset is completely different; I feel God *restoring* me. My voice was deeper. While driving and simply speaking, my sister burst into tears at what God had done. She was extremely happy, and she prayed; she released a Word from God, which was to *"Trust the Process"; God is going to bring you out and fully restore your mind."

I get home, I feel new, like learning everything all over again. My mother would consistently check on me to make sure I'm ok, pray for me and encourage me. I would just seek God each day. I felt nothing but freedom. I didn't have much to worry about at this time because God was supplying my needs according to His riches and glory.

I began to be productive at home and just started cleaning up. I still had mental issues; it was just like when I was cleaning up the neighborhood and started losing my mind. Unfortunately, I began to clean up even place that didn't belong to me. I would begin to take things that if they were torn or ripped or I considered old, I would trash them. I made the mistake of throwing away Nellie's( my other sisters) blanket that she sleeps under. I replaced it with a new blanket that we kept in the closet. In my head, I was doing a good deed but this was not the case to her. When she got home and found out, it sparked a huge argument.

The argument eventually led her to call the police. I called my pastor, and he sent someone to get me. After he finished preaching at His north Memphis location, he took me out to His favorite restaurant, picadellys. He gave me wisdom, treated me to a good meal and got in touch with my other sister, Cora and she came to the restaurant. They worked out a place to put me in in the meantime, which turned out to be a place called Crestwyn temporarily, another mental health facility.

This place was exactly like lakeside, just a tiny bit higher on the socioeconomic scale. They take really good care of you. From 3 meals a day to a gym to play basketball to an outside park-looking area, they nurse you back to a healthy mindset greatly. I don't have anything negative to say about a mental health facility; it can be a bit of a stigma, but the help you get is priceless. And the most priceless thing they do is keep bibles on hand. For me, it was to "*Trust the Process*" even in this place. All I did was again, ask for a bible and read it. There was healing and peace that surpassed all understanding like before.

I learned there are people in the housing market who simply partner with these facilities to have a home to stay in when people get released. It's a business, and I was the client. I became the person who would choose which home I wanted to be in after having a meeting with the different homeowners. I chose a woman who was saved, and we connected almost immediately on a spiritual level. The first thing she stated, I would almost say prophetically, is that eventually, I would help a lot of young people; once this process is over and God brings me out, then I will help other people. So they give a recommendation for a new psychiatrist downtown to work with once I'm settled.

I get released, I'm taken to Ms. G by a taxi, I feel free again, I'm back in the free world. My mind is clearer again. I get welcomed humbly into this home. I get shown my room and get acclimated to this new house. This was all new to me. Once again, I felt like Job in the Bible, meaning God "allowed" me to go through this because I needed to see a world I had never seen before, especially in the *"imperfectly perfect"* world I was in previously.

I shared the room with a vessel named Mr. Miller. A saved Caucasian man and a steward in the Word. I enjoyed being here. It was similar to being in a mental health facility, but I had more freedom. I do the same here, ask for a Bible, and I read it daily.

After about a month here, I was ready to go back to work, I felt my mind was clear and I continue to feel God *restoring* me. I messaged my boss, and he said I was clear to come back whenever I was ready. He's the best and helped vouch and provide all the resources needed. Even resources I didn't even know existed that the government offered.

I come back to the office for the first time, and I realized something, nothing changed! The normal operations were still going on. I learned something, it doesn't matter what you go through; life still goes on.

Life doesn't stop just because you are going through a tough time; you just have to press on and endure. Because the race is not to the swift, but is he who endures to the end! So don't rush the process. Take your time and trust God. Trust the Process. You have to keep going. So, I began to start getting acclimated again. They work with me at a very slow pace, and they don't put anything on me that is more than I can bear.

After about a month of returning to work, I returned home with my family, and Nellie allowed me back in. I leave the rooming house and start getting back acclimated to life at home and returning to work daily at a slow pace.

I felt like a kid again and even a little bit spoiled with how many times my mother would come open my door and just set a plate of food down. It was joyful, and just took time to get on my knees and thank God for everything!

So I am taken to go see a new psychiatrist that the mental health facility recommended, who turns out to be a spiritual person. She was more concerned with getting me off stimulant medication and getting the stimulant medication out of my system, which, in her experience, exacerbates the problems.

She put me on a shot called "Invega", which decreased over time to help wean off the medications that were in my system.

Each day was clearer and clearer after each shot every month. Every visit was amazing; this was truly God allowing me to get the right psychiatrist. This journey was partly natural and spiritual. I began to seek the Lord even more. As you seek Him, the Holy Spirit will guide you. I said, I *know I can be free from this, but God, how? Was there a certain type of prayer needed, as my uncle mentioned?* I prayed and asked God again, "*What is my purpose?*" *How do I fully break free from this bondage?* It's not a one-time thing or formula. It's a process. God was plainly revealing to me I had to "*Trust the Process*".

I then had another divine encounter. My sister Cora asked to take me to a "healing" and "deliverance" ministry. The Lord led me to be a part of a smaller church for a season. (I thank God for her, she was always there for me throughout my whole journey). We went there, and I didn't utter a word, but all I could hear was these anointed vessels praying in "tongues" (God's heavenly language), just like how my sister prays and how I hear my adoptive mom prays. The pastor looked at me and kept praying like God was revealing some things regarding me to her (This later turned out to be true). I walked up there and they got around me and began to pray and pull out this pool( a mat with scriptures on it). They said to me, "*We're about to walk you through some deliverance. It will help break the chains and curses off you.*" They gave me a "prayer manual", which contained prayers to break generational curses and a multitude of other things that I couldn't even comprehend, and for healing and deliverance, it doesn't happen overnight. It's a process as well. Remember it's God ultimately doing the work in you. I received Jesus Christ as my Lord and Savior again; I simply re-dedicated myself which is common on the

Christian journey. Just like I spoke about mental health issues over my life, they had me speak the opposite, binding and loosing these generational curses and mental health disorders off of my life. I definitely felt God's presence in this.

I walked out of the church one day with a clear mind; I said in my head, "I feel restored". I kept coming back, and my mind became clearer each time I walked out of there. Finally, after a while of the natural process and the spiritual process, which is psychiatrist visits and church visits, I feel a chapter of my life was completed. I felt like a warrior in God's army; I Won this battle. I didn't give up. So, anyone who questions your praise to God, tell them your testimony. They don't know what you've been through and how God brought you out. He deserves the highest praise!

*"Trust the Process."*

*Chapter 13*

# Spirit-filled

There were very calming things I was instructed to do, like just go walking at the park, and go to the gym. I did yoga for some time. I ate healthier. The most effective thing is I would speak with those close to me who could minister to my mind. Some of these natural things helped mentally and continue to be apart of my process. I can't say this enough, there are times you just need someone to talk to, just their voice can minister to your mind, body and spirit to help with any form of anxiety that tries to attack your mind. The Bible says,

*"casting all your cares [all your anxieties, all your worries, and all your concerns, once and for all] on Him, for He cares about you [with deepest affection, and watches over you very carefully]."*

It took a few months' sessions with my new psychiatrist to wean off any stimulant medication that was in my system, so this was a time of patience, so I encourage anyone to *Trust the Process*, don't rush it. I went to church more and learned more about God and the teachings of Jesus Christ. Learning about Him and His learning His word never stops; we will be learning about Him until we leave this earth.

And to God be the glory, I never lost the job that I was blessed with. I returned back to work and got acclimated to work again. They worked me at a slower pace until I get back up to speed. This is to encourage those in leadership to make sure they understand that mental health is a major factor in the workplace. Keep in mind that some don't know their condition can be temporary, so be sure your employees are provided with reasonable accommodations in the meantime to help them in the process.

I began to pray and ask God again, *"What is my purpose?"* The pastor and leaders of the deliverance ministry spoke prophetically and mentioned that I needed to receive the baptism of the Holy Spirit with evidence of speaking in tongues. It's a gift from the Lord. It's the same gift my adoptive mother and my sister have. The Bible says,

*"But ye shall receive power, after that the Holy Ghost is come upon you: and ye shall be witnesses unto me both in Jerusalem, and in all Judæa, and in Samaria, and unto the uttermost part of the earth."*

I said, *"I want this gift."* You should desire this, too, once you mature in the faith.

Therefore, I began to read more about it and then I asked God to bless me with the Gift of the Holy Spirit with the evidence of speaking in tongues. The church and its Saints were determined to help me receive it. They loved God's people and truly wanted to see people get saved and go through the process of salvation and get whatever God has for them.

So always get to know God for yourself an and not base your relationship with Him on anyone else. The saints walked me through the process and have me to say, *"Thank you, Jesus",* repeatedly until I was filled with power, my voice shifted, and I started speaking in tongues boldly. I couldn't stop speaking in this language at first. Yes, I had to be filled the old-fashioned way, just like the older saints.

It was a celebration, I received the free gift, the baptism of the Holy Spirit.

But then, just when I think it's all over, even after I receive this power, the journey continues. The enemy comes even harder to attack my mind now that I'm closer to my purpose.

## Chapter 14

# The FBI Encounter

Things appear to be going well again for me. I've returned back to work, slowly getting acclimated to the technical environment again. I'm back home and rebuilding relationships with family. I'm going to church consistently because that's where God wants me. I even received the gift of the Holy Spirit. I worked well with my psychiatrist to get weaned off stimulant medication so my mind would be clear. All appears to be going well over the next few months. So, after one of my last psychiatrist visits everything appeared to be fine. My psychiatrist said *"there's no need to continue coming if everything is back to normal."* This reminds of a scripture.

*Jesus said, They that are whole have no need of the physician, but they that are sick: I came not to call the righteous, but sinners to repentance.*

So I have my last appointment with my psychiatrist and everything is going well. But maybe a little over a month after things are going so well, my mind begins to become distorted. *My reality begins to shift, I became disconnected from reality.*

I begin to have to mental thoughts of working with the Federal Bureau of Investigations(FBI). I wasn't able to think clearly at how serious an organization such as the FBI is. So I have a brief encounter with them stopping by their office with my work badge on and a Bible claiming I want to work with them. I go through the rest of the day and receive a text from my manager later that evening stating they received a report from the FBI. So going forward I was not allowed on government property till further notice. I didn't know what to do or say so I had to contact my sister Cora the next day, she had me to come over and we talked about it. Eventually she decided to pray with me regarding the situation. I didn't want to lose my job over something so foolish. Thanks be to God, I receive an update from my new manager that I would be put on leave status, "with pay" until they finish the investigation. All I could do is shout.

So my sister takes me back to the psychiatrist. They diagnosed me with *"Psychosis"*. I'm put back on the Invega shot again, which helped bring my mind back to a normal reality.

Time goes by, days turn to weeks, weeks to months. I have tons of anxiety but I'm thankful at the same time. Although I'm not working, I am getting normal pay every two weeks as if I was working. Each month I visit the psychiatrist with my sister or my pops(my sisters dad). He became like a father to me during this time of my life. I begin to call on him almost every day and God allowed to be in my life more at this time. Naturally he filled the father wound void I was always missing, but spiritually God filled the father wound as well.

I'm more stable and clear minded after each visit. A whole year goes by and I'm just waiting, thinking, and constantly getting my shot every month. Just pondering on what's to come from this process. I would text my new manager every month for a while and he would always respond, "no update". So eventually I became at peace, I began to seek the Lord. I began to just read my Bible periodically everyday, it almost seemed like there was nothing left to do except be patient and as the psalmist David says, "*wait on the Lord*".

So at this time, I feel fully at peace and my mind is clear again. I feel totally *restored*. I just wanted to begin telling people my story and also witness to people the goodness of God during this process. Although medicated, I become at peace with the fact that I might just be on this medication for a long time or forever. This is what my psychiatrist stated may be the case in one of my visits. Regardless of the outcome, we all are believers and know that Gods knows the plan he has for us.

So one day I decided to start filling my time by going to the stores and I started witnessing to people. I start evangelizing. I felt purposeful. Everyday was a goal of just talking with people about the Lord and possibly winning a soul, and getting that opportunity to tell people my testimony. It was great, it kept me going for this time.

So it easily became a normal routine. I would wake up everyday and just start early by sometimes taking a walk or going to the gym, then come home shower and start my day. I would simply visit a multitude of stores and have a plethora of opportunities to meet different people. It was great, the feeling of simply walking in purpose, sharing the goodness of God with people.

Then one day, after almost 2 years I receive an update via mail from my job. It lays out in full detail everything that happened.

Then the letter stated I needed to justify my actions with a response, preferably from a medical professional. Thanks be to God I had a psychiatrist who helped me through the whole process. They drafted up a nice letter detailing me being under there care for the past two years. After waiting about a month later, they made a decision. The letter was sufficient enough to justify my actions. They give me instructions on my return back to work procedures.

So about two weeks before I start back work. I get a call from another "new" manager. He turned out to be a real cool laid back manager who doesn't judge you. He helped me through the process of getting back on the job successfully. So after the two weeks, I'm back on the job, they work with me at a very slow pace to get up to speed on the environment. My mind is clear and I'm stable, thanks to the Lord. I begin to get acclimated back to some of the technical tasks I was doing in the past. Then as time goes by, they see how well I'm doing, they start to give me new tasks. I begin doing those well with no problems then they start getting me more involved with the team. Close to a years time goes by and I receive an email from our Director, my first manager.

He drafted up a very nice email and and cc'd some of the managers. He summarized all the work I had been doing based on a meeting with him and my current manager, he gave me kudos for all the hard work I had done after returning back with no issues to report. So he gave me a huge shoutout. I was extremely blessed by this that God brought me such a long way and things are going so well for me. God is good.

## Chapter 15

# Restored

I still keep going to the psychiatrist every month for updates, and everything is going fine. I'm back at work, doing the tasks they asked me to do. My relationships with family are good. I purchased my first house so now I'm a homeowner. I find a new church home where I feel God has led me to after moving. My mind is stable, and I haven't gotten a hint of distortion or any symptoms of any disorder at all after over 2 years time has passed. I feel God has truly *restored* me, and this is the process he wanted me to go through, even with medication, which is the shot called "Invega".

I eventually need to air things out, although things are going well. So, my sister, Cora, recommends I get a therapist. I move forward with this and she helps me find a good one. I scheduled to meet with him and make it consistent for a few months. I talked with him about "everything." It helped tremendously; it was apart of my healing process throughout all of this.

Here is a list of things that worked for me through this process. Try these yourself.

Psychiatry: Ask the Lord to lead you to the right psychiatrist, this has a major impact on the process. It's ok to shop around until you find the right one. Also, there are programs that don't require any insurance and it's fully paid for, you just have to do your research.

The Spiritual: Take time to get to know God for yourself in His Word. I recommend investing in a KJV Bible since it's the universal standard. The Lord will lead you to another version that breaks down the Word a little easier in due time. Read the through entire New Testament. In the Old Testament, I recommend, Psalms, Proverbs & my 2nd favorite book Ecclesiastes. If you're new in the faith, start with the Gospel of John, my first favorite book.

Find a church home: Take time to visit different churches and find one that fits best for you, there are many. I'm sure God will lead you to the right one. Being in the company of like believers has a tremendous effect of your mental health, and there's nothing like community.

Communication: God knows who and when to place people in your life who can speak or minister to you.

Sometimes it's just the sound of someone's voice or you being able to talk with someone that brings peace to your mind. This can be family, church members, friends, or coworkers. It doesn't have to be a lot of people, just a few can help.

Physical Health: Take time and go to the gym even if you don't feel like it. Getting there is the hardest part but once your there, go ahead and knock it out. Gyms with classes are good, like boxing, kickboxing, or CrossFit.

Take time to go walking at the park or around the neighborhood. It's good to get out in nature and let the sun shine on you sometimes, this can be very peaceful and take time to talk with Lord on the walk.

Take a yoga class. I did this for a month and it was very calming for the mind.

Sounds: Take time to listen to different music that speaks to your spirit or helps make you feel better. One tremendous thing that helped me is motivational videos or sermons on YouTube. A few voices that helped me via YouTube are Steve Harvey, Denzel Washington, Les Brown, Dr. Myles Munroe, Billy Graham, Oprah Winfrey, Eric Thomas, Ray Lewis and Creflo Dollar. Find who works for you.

Writing: I have a Gmail, so on my google drive I created a document where I journaled. I wrote "everything" that I could think of from my earliest memories in life all the way till what I feel today. And see if it doesn't turn into a nice "autobiography" and hit the US best sellers list.

Write your story. This may be the vision God is planting in you also for a book to be published. You never know where your book may take you and you could help millions with your testimony.

Therapy: Take time to seek out a therapist, this will help you air things outs and talk about everything, even when there are very private things you wouldn't want to tell anybody, a therapist is actually a good person to tell these things.

On the job: Communicate with your manager or lead on your mental health. They have reasonable accommodations that help. If needed, have your psychiatrist draft up a letter detailing some reasonable accommodations. One thing that they put in my letter was task management, they put step by step instructions together to make my tasks easier to understand. Also, the letter detailed having more 15-minute breaks in the morning and afternoon.

Alone time: There are times when you will be all alone. Know this, God is right there with you, have a talk with him. There are times when there doesn't need to be any music, or YouTube or people talking with you, just have a little talk with Jesus.

Live: At the end of it all, live your life, and enjoy it, find something fun that you like to do. Trouble won't last always. Going through mental health battles is a process but know that God will see you through.

I thank God for allowing me to *Trust the Process*, and He's doing the same for you.

So the process for me has been, to stay on medication for now and guess what? _It's ok, there's nothing wrong with having to be on medication, if it works for you, keep on trusting the process God has for you._ I now embrace the fact that I'm on medication. If you remain on it forever, that's fine. If I myself or you somehow are blessed to come off of medication, that's fine too. Regardless of which way life takes you, trust God. Trust His plan. Trust His Process.

# Invitation to Salvation

After all this, my overall purpose is to bring people into the knowledge of Jesus Christ; God wants us to help people get saved. This is technically God's ultimate purpose for everyone. In addition to this purpose, everyone has their own unique purpose God has placed in them. Apart of my purpose was revealed in the mental health facility when God planted the vision of me becoming an author and writing my story to help people and bring them to God. That's what this whole journey in life is about, it's about Him. The Bible says,

*"For God so loved the world, that he gave his only begotten Son, that whosoever believeth in him should not perish, but have everlasting life."*

I couldn't finish this book without extending an invitation for you to be saved. It is very simple, and it's free.

**Romans 10:9**

*"If thou shalt confess with thy mouth the Lord Jesus, and shalt believe in thine heart that God hath raised him from the dead, thou shalt be saved."*

Remember that God is Sovereign and in control of everything. It does not matter what you are going through or what you have gone through, because we all have a story. My hope and advice is that you continually trust Him, I repeat; "trust … the … process" and He will see you through. You can overcome anything, you got this.

"Stay Focused"

If you need someone to walk with you through this process or for any inquiries. Contact me here.

Email: Jeremiah.i.cain@gmail.com

# Notes

_____

_____

_____

_____

_____

_____

_____

_____

_____

_____

_____

_____

_____

_____

_____

_____

_____

_____

_____

# Notes

# About the Book

This book pertains to those who have suffered from the stigma and acceptance of issues with mental Health. It is a story detailing the life of a boy who was born with a purpose. During this time, he goes on a journey from trying to escape from a mental health diagnoses to having a purpose; which is to help others who have similar issues overcome theirs. It is a story about him growing up as an adopted child who was gifted. A gifted child who graduates from the school system and begins a career in technology. After years of a successful career in IT (Information Technology), he discovers that he is adopted and reconnects with his biological family. Shortly after, he stumbles across his mental diagnosis. After years in bondage of multiple disorders, he has several divine encounters that lead him to Christ and helped bring him closer to his purpose. The purpose and plan that was predestined before he was born.

# About the Author

Jeremiah is an upcoming author who is making an impact in the mental health community, and what he would rather call the "Community of Gifted Children and Adults". He has a background in the Information Technology; helping others with technical support, teaching and cybersecurity. His life is circled around supporting and encouraging others with his gift.

Made in the USA
Columbia, SC
13 July 2025